— ROLLING STACK

TONBRIDGF

Remem

LINTEL

Gillian Allnutt was born in 1949 in London but spent half of her childhood in Newcastle upon Tyne. In 1988 she returned to live in the North East. Before that, she read Philosophy and English at Cambridge and then spent the next 17 years living mostly in London, working mostly as a part-time teacher in further and adult education but also as a performer, publisher, journalist and freelance editor. From 1983 to 1988 she was Poetry Editor at *City Limits* magazine.

She has published five collections of poetry: *Spitting the Pips Out* (Sheba, 1981) and *Beginning the Avocado* (Virago, 1987), and from Bloodaxe Books, *Blackthorn* (1994), *Nantucket and the Angel* (1997) and *Lintel* (2001), the last two both shortlisted for the T.S. Eliot Prize. *Lintel* is the Poetry Book Society Choice for Spring 2001.

Gillian Allnutt co-edited *The New British Poetry* (Paladin, 1988) and is the author of *Berthing: A Poetry Workbook* (National Extension College/Virago, 1991). She currently teaches creative writing and literature in adult education and works as a writer in schools.

Gillian Allnutt

◉

LINTEL

BLOODAXE BOOKS

Copyright © Gillian Allnutt 2001

ISBN: 1 85224 547 6

First published 2001 by
Bloodaxe Books Ltd,
Highgreen,
Tarset,
Northumberland NE48 1RP.

Bloodaxe Books Ltd acknowledges
the financial assistance of Northern Arts.

R26210
821.914

Cover printing by J. Thomson Colour Printers Ltd, Glasgow.

Printed in Great Britain by
Cromwell Press Ltd, Trowbridge, Wiltshire.

For my father
Gordon Terry Allnutt

Acknowledgements

Acknowledgements are due to the editors of the following publications in which some of these poems first appeared: *The Cúirt Journal, Kunapipi, Mslexia, The North, Poetry Ireland Review, Poetry London, Poetry Review, The Rialto, The Tabla Book of New Verse 1998* and *Tears in the Fence.*

'Healer' (under the title 'Like the heart') was commissioned by Hyphen-21 for Poems for the Waiting Room, a scheme to display poems in waiting rooms in hospitals, medical centres, doctors' and dentists' surgeries nationwide. 'The Silk Light of Advent' was broadcast by BBC Radio 3 as part of *An Advent Anthology* in December 1996.

I'd like to thank Northern Arts for a Tyrone Guthrie Award in 1995 and a Writer's Award in 1998.

I'd also like to thank Margaret Wilkinson and everyone who comes, or has come, to the women's writing workshop, Writing from the Inside Out, at Newcastle University's Centre for Lifelong Learning. Many of the poems in this collection started in Inside Out sessions.

Contents

On the Dark Side of the Moon

I hear the stars exploding all around me with a soft wet sound.

I hear the exasperated wind.

I hear my feet rasp. How they long to rest themselves on moss.

I hear sand turn to less

and less than itself. I hear my tongue,

stone, hollowing.

I hear the earth, a clay pot on a wheel.

I hear the soul's

song, what is near.

I hear the waterholes, the stricken cattle of the air.

The Makings of Marmalade

unripe oranges in silk-lined sacks
sow-bristle brushes
china jugs of orange-washing water
one big bowl
pith-paring knives, one for each woman
a mountain of sugar, poured slowly
a small Sevillian well
songsheets against the tedium, in parts
pine cones for burning
silver spoons for licking up the lost bits
a seven-gallon pot
a waxed circle, a sellophane circle, elastic
small pieces of toast

SARAH'S LAUGHTER

Scheherazade

He is languid as a fed lion.
She in her salt and sackcloth gown is gone
into a wilderness of wind at noon

where the wonderful covered well of tales
is a dry waterhole
or a bell

abandoned. What is the sound at noon
of silence in a grain
of sand? It may be what is borne

by her beyond the hollowed bone of thought,
the loud elaborated heart,
the salt

and sack-
cloth shadow begging briefly at her back,
her Bedouin back.

Sarah's Laughter

Sarah's laughter's sudden, like a hurdle, like an old loud crow
that comes out of the blue.

The graceful men at the makeshift table –
there, in the shade of the tree, in the heat of the day, in Bethel –

look up from the all too tender veal,
the buttermilk, the three small

cakes of meal she's made them. For her husband
Abraham, she's sifted, shaped them in her old dry hand.

Good Lord, no. Laugh? Not I. For Sarah's suddenly afraid.
She did what she could

when she sent him in to that Hagar, handmaid, then,
yes, then dealt hardly with her, only then

let her bide with the lad
Ishmael. A sturdy lad.

It's hidden, the hurt, like a hard little bird in the tent
of her heart. She's tended it

To Lot's Wife

At least we don't know your name. It might have been

one that meant halt, handmaid, hard to insult
in the old Hebraic tongue.

Silt-white, anonymous, you might have been
any woman, any

one of us who, turning, turns
attention

to the bed, to linen, to belonging
bare and dear

enough to hang onto.

Look, you've already lost your daughters.

Later they'll lie with their father, their future
laid down.

Look at the city of salt and exult.

Lighter than laughter you are at the last
and alone.

Annunciation

I was alone at the well.
I was doused in shadow and in deed.
My yoke lay on the ground, waiting.
I cannot say what I mean.
I was come upon.
I was going to carry the water to my espoused man,
Joseph, of the house of David.

A Letter from Marie-Claire to Her Sister

Paris, February 1910

Now I can see the unevenness of the wall and the place
where the icon was.

She called it *La Vieille*.

Mary's dress, a greenish blue, was like the sea.

I wish I were in Dieppe, still walking on the grey sea-wall.

I wish I were in Dieppe, still counting the cobbles.

I wish I were in Dieppe, asleep with her in the low dark room,
still waiting for the boat to come.

I hear her now: *Claire, Marie-Claire,*
bring me my pearl. They buried it with her.

They buried her in the sea with its great grey swell.

When I got back here I was ill.

Guillaume's Loom, Hastings, 1080

I made a loom for Mathilda, my English daughter.
'Mathilde!' I called. I wanted to show her
The strong clay rings I'd made to hold the thread
As hard and near as I held her. I wasn't proud
Of the rest – a rough affair of stick and thole
Cut from the worst English wood, I think hazel,
And English wool.

Margaret Heslop on the morning
of her father's funeral, February 1627

I am left to winter light and the will of God
now Father is dead.
Magda, the wooden-haired doll, is with me, laid
on the windowsill in her wooden bed.
I'll take the grace and loneliness of morning with me when we go
among the dark yews to my father's burial and know
my being alone here is – well, loveliness.
Being here in my black wool dress.
Martha put the lead-weights in my hair
before she lit the fire
this morning. So it won't curl.
Those who are to come to Father's funeral
will crowd in curiously. One day
a married, meek-haired Margaret will come, a long time after me.

Her Father Walks Over Eggleston Moor

I will take her the sunlight caught in my coat, its smell of wool.
I will take her the boat-on-wheels –
I dare say Martha will be good enough to mend the smaller sail.
I will take her the sound of the sea that has crossed the hills
Without its shell.

Her Father in the Patients' Garden,
Newcastle Borough Lunatic Asylum, 1919

I am not lost. I harbour my loneliness here
By the larkspur. Here, where the hand of my daughter,
Margaret's hand in hard love, took my elbow –
The smell of the ward's in my hair.
Behind me now, the black clocktower, the wall –
O God, our... God, reported missing and presumed, etcetera,
When they built that wall.
I'll take my soul and sixpence when I go.
I'll go to Muriel, though she is laid
Aside. My mother, Dad, my mother's... Margaret said.
The stones of the path in the patients' garden –
Narrow then wide, narrow then wide.

Carmody Visits the Lock-keeper's Daughter

Those who made lace were here before me.
My father and mother forget sometimes to walk in front of me.
Last night I heard the linnet sing
and now there is the dull canal of coming
here. I dream I bear my own black boat upon my back
and can't abandon it.
I'll buy her linen thread to caulk the seams of it.

In Old Age He Visits Eugenie's Grave

Here is the pocket in which, all my life, I have carried her
small silver casket. Here is the casket.
Look, how it catches at light, like a heart, like water.
'Ca' the Yowes' she sang to me under the alder that wet night.
She sang like Kathleen Ferrier.
There are flowers hereabout, in the mist, in the smirr.
I've brought her a basket of eyebright,
brought them from the moors.

My Camberwell Grandmother Before Her Marriage

The upholsterer's late.
He'll say that he couldn't get over the road at New Cross Gate.
A little man from Mile End, moth-eaten.
Must have grown up on bread and gin.
How did Father get hold of him? I don't know.
I wish he had not. For now
There's no end to the mending of Mother's old chairs, the ones
She chose from Dickens and Jones.
I wish she'd gone out of this life
Like a light, like Elijah's wife
Herself, two flaming chairs, a double chariot of fire.
That's how I'd like to remember Mother.
Not, as I now must, waiting in all afternoon. I might have been
In Worthing. Mother, of course, would be gone
To the corner of Jerningham Road
To choose bricks from the yard
For the outhouse Father began in nineteen hundred and six.
Mother loved choosing bricks.
I suppose they would meet, herself, the upholsterer,
Waiting to cross between motor-cars.
She'd notice the bodkin stuck in his hat.
She used to tell Father about it at night
In their room. *Did you notice*
The bodkin? she'd ask, undoing her bodice
And all those buttons, his buttons,
Her buttons of bone.

The English Widow

(after 'La Dame dans le Train ou la Veuve' by Léon Spilliaert)

My life that day was – lank, borne.
I was led to a bench in the waiting-room.
I was led into the garden.
My life with him had been hard-won.
Parts of it, like small planks, fitted together.
Later I needed a woollen gown for all weathers.
It was mildewed with mud at the hem.
'Weeds' my mother said in my mind.
I walked out in the autumn wind.
I walked to the station somewhere in Belgium.
It had been my husband's homely land, then mine.
I abandoned the portrait Léon had made of the garden.
Apples lay on the ground, in the long grass, hidden.
A low wind hovered over them.
To what end were all things given?

The Silk Light of Advent

Mara sighs over the silks laid out on the rosewood windowsill.
She would rather look into the fire.
It is terribly hard to decide when the garden is dead.
In December the lake is dumb.
There are no leaves left and no wind left to stir them.
Later in life she will say that the light on the Somme was like
     that then.
Mara sighs over the skeins.
She is neither girl nor woman.
Her brother is in uniform.
There is no one left to walk with in the morning.
Her mother has always left her alone.
The newspaper's forbidden.
The angel will be embroidered, soon, by evensong.
After that there'll be no more sewing.
In the beginning needles were made of bone.
The angel will come in the afternoon.
Later in life she will know the value of precision.
At two o'clock in the afternoon she will say again and again.
Her brother will not be missing then.
He writes he is learning to smoke and polish buttons.
She will get up from the fire.
She'll walk slowly back to the windowsill.
She'll know then that the angel's hands are dumb.
The eyes are gone.
There are sockets of silk she will never embroider for him.
The lake is dry, like bone.
The angel is terribly beautiful.
She won't be able to cry.

In the Fens   1920

the two of us then   as if *the two of them*
unfallen apple blossom
dabble of light   white muslin gown

plate of plain bread and butter
and the may   must've come early that year
to Grantchester

to that tea garden   now and then   no road
and nowhere now to hide
the pollarded

willow   the Cam
the abrupt stump of the Somme
the wounded in the university garden

the wind
the unending   black almost   bloodless land
I have found

Anchorage

In Julian's alone unlettered hand
love takes the hard ground

dust of oak-
gall and the quill, the history of the soul. It breaks

an April into tiny unprotected revelations
of its own. It makes bone

flower like blackthorn.

THE ROAD HOME

Awkward Things (1)

the albatross
my father's deafness
dust under the bed
the distance, now, between
the eye of the needle
and the thread
the wings in the cupboard

Awkward Things (2)

Ely, the ship of the fens in its fastness
the camel and the dromedary
Christmas
that bits of it are in Latin
that we'll be charged to go in
that we're 'crossing the desert in a pram'
that we persist in going on

The Road Home

It is the road to God
that matters now, the ragged road, the wood.

And if you will, drop pebbles here and there
like Hansel, Gretel, right where

they'll shine
in the wilful light of the moon.

You won't be going back to the hut
where father, mother plot

the *cul de sac* of the world
in a field

that's permanently full
of people

looking for a festival
of literature, a fairy tale,

a feathered
nest of brothers, sisters. Would

that first world, bared now to the word
God, wade

with you, through wood, into the weald and weather
of the stars?

Village in County Durham, 1998

And now an angel passes like a bus, its scarlet side
too soiled with old advertisement

to be of use. Where men are
knocking down the old shirt factory

with ball and chain in the short December dusk, it will
break down.

In summer when the factory floor was strewn with dust –
it must have been asbestos – and the door stove in

again, the kids, their pockets and an old pram
loaded to the brim with apples, came

to lob for dear life
till the windows lay like lustres in the sun.

Now, where the wings, in late December undistinguished as the
        sides of
buses, stall

there is a scattering of roof and ritual.

Looking at Chagall's 'Solitude' on a Windy Night

And now as the angel flies away over the small Russian town –
that'll be Vitebsk –
there is no protection.
Neither the cow nor the man has the heart
to work up a tune on the old violin –
oh, one of those wedding tunes you'd hear at the back of the little
        town –
nor will the man again hold the moon in his hand like an always
almost lost solution or a dream.
Ladybird, ladybird, fly away home.
The man and the cow are sitting down.
The man holds the Torah in its tight scroll
like a parasol.

And now as the wind howls over this one-in-a-hundred-small-towns
        town –
something lamentable, something less, though it is tonal, than
a half-remembered tune –
now I lay me down to sleep.
May I be sheltered, hid, as if from the steppe
at the back of my unwed heart.
If there's a wedding, it flies away over the foothills of the Pennines.

The river, Yenisey

We do not make the journey any more.
Most of us work. That is a way of forgetting.
We do not speak of the nameless river.
It was an autumnal river, fast, rising.
It was full of the rain that had wetted our heads
         and shoulders.
It waited for the empty cradle we set upon the water.
Our cradles are full now. Our cupboards are full.
Our speech is meaningful, like money.
We are mute, literate.
We are in love with our own imagination, the name
         of the river, Yenisey.
We know nothing of namelessness, nothing.
Nothing, in due course, comes to us.
We came to the river, as I remember, the cradle
         scrubbed and serviceable.
Sorrow caught up with us, sorrow in its shawl.
We set it afloat.
Now we are lost among satisfactions.
Now we are literate.

Barclays Bank and Lake Baikal

The bank walks in at half past seven, dressed and unembarrassed
by its sponsorship of Beethoven, the best

of music, *Hammerklavier*, here in its own town
Darlington.

Demidenko, Nikolai, in concert, self-exiled,
walks out of another world

like one who's wandered, handkerchief in hand, into the town
to watch the hammer of the auctioneer come down

and then, instead, plays Beethoven
as if he were alone.

He looks like Silas Marner so intent upon his two thick leather
        bags of gold
he lost the world

we live in: cough, cold, cufflink and the ache and pain
of bone.

It looks as if the light, Siberian, is breaking slowly over Lake Baikal,
as if our ship of fools

and bankers, borne upon the waters
of a bare

adagio, may founder in a quite uncalled for and unsponsored
sea of solitude.

But not tonight, dour Demidenko, dealer in another world's
dear gold –

for Darlington's recalled. At ten to ten
the bank picks up its leather bag, walks out again.

Advent in the Cathedral

1 *Carol Service*

Lord, they are filling the aisles with gait and shuffle.
Lord, we have laid on carols

for all those with learning difficulties. We are an incorrigible
people,

Lord, we are linguistically charitable,
we are a Barbie doll. We have laid on carols for all

the disabled,
those whose faces are turned to the wall of the world –

poor likeness of, poor dear approximation to, the ideal.
Lord, our beauty is visible

or else, among the elevated gutters of the soul,
we're gargoyles all.

We'd lose our nerve at that, Lord, and not less than all
the gait and shuffle

of political correctness,
cleverness,

our old credentials.
Lord, we'd lose our credibility to these undecorated walls.

2 *Altarcloth*

Because this bone blue bare embroidered altarcloth
stiff, almost, as an old truth,

as the self – holds
good, the sea stopped in its folds,

I stand, as if I'd stood for ever at the water's
edge, alone and waiting for

the one inheritance
of absence.

This morning, the moon at flood, its cold salt
light

incomparable.
Still

what I love's the equivocal thought of the sea,
the sepulchre

of that small chapel on a point
in Dorset.

I imagine St Aldhelm, steeped in prayer, in doubt
stepped out

over the salt-dry sill
of the soul

into the cold incomparable air.

Arvo Pärt in Concert, Durham Cathedral, November 1998

Sea-otters will be calving soon about the Farnes.

Perhaps you'll go there, in your coat, tonight.
Perhaps you'll go to Coldingham

or Lindisfarne, or, landlocked, wait, as if
you too were

sandstone: wounded, worn by wind, rain, light.

O Lord, enlighten my heart which evil desires have darkened

where the imperturbable pillars stand.

For you have fidgeted through sermons.

Hard to sit still with all your insufficiency about you, isn't it?

But you will listen through your permeable skin as if
this music were

slow wounding, swearing in, osmosis.

Ebba, abbess of Coldingham, will find her nuns forsaken, fidgeting,

but you, as Cuthbert, suffering for all, will make straight
for the sea, to stand all night
waist-deep in it,

in praise and prayer,

in fret, is it, or under the stars' bare
scattering of thorns –

O Lord, give me tears and remembrance of death, and
        contrition –

until dawn. When you will kneel down on the sand.
Sea-otters will come to warm you then.

But you must be as sandstone.

Make of this music an Inner Farne where you may stand alone.

For it *is* Farne, from Celtic *ferann*, meaning land,

where monks will dig a well for you of wild fresh water,
where you'll find not wheat but barley growing on bare ground,
where you will build a wall so high around
your oratory, you'll know the sky, it only
a while

as instrumental, wearing-in of wind and water. Listen

then, you'll find your own skin, salt, intact
as Cuthbert after centuries of wandering, still
permeable –

O Lord, forsake me not –

and one, as Arvo Pärt in his coat, will stand before
the orchestra, the choir, as if he too had only now
walked out of water

new, renewable, knowing the comfort of sea-otters.

INISI IKEEL

Strangeness

I

May it rise again
like the moon

from the sea
at the mouth of the Liffey

blurred by cloud
saffron coloured

for those who walk swiftly in darkness there
by the water.

II

May it stagger like silence
broken – by the glance

of bat's wing,
one dog barking

in Monaghan,
the pother and throng of my own

thought bothering
to put the boot in.

III

May it dispel
me and all

my affordable castles of stone.
May it come as famine,

faerie queene or fine
acidic rain –

or come at all, as if it were the soul's full
creel.

Meditation

I said to my soul: be still and wait
where the light green sediment collects

at the lake's near edge.
An old red lifebelt hangs in silence, sedge-

still. Still the long rope,
loosely gathered, loops

on its cast-iron post
like hope, at rest.

Held To

And now a little wind but little wind and stone and green –
grave-green

the pod of flowered-
already reed

or sedge –
and now, at water's edge,

a leap and tipple – toad, alone, moves
now, reminds me of

the little tinie page,
the page

in *Matty Groves*, who ran to give the game away
on New Year's Day

and now, but for the barest grace of balladry, go I
too hurriedly

beyond
this borderland,

this little hoard of stone, pod, wind
in the hand

that would hold tipple-
still

to

Annaghmakerrig

(for Bernard and Mary Loughlin)

It is the lake, whatever you make of it, lighter
    than Baikal, less alone.

It is the swallow that sped through my room by mistake
    like the sparrow that speeds from dark to dark
        through the meadhall.

It is the dining-table, long on its way to Liverpool,
    a *Lusitania* of laughter.

It is wit and water and that bit crack
    that's Geordie for *craic*.

It is gin and tonic.

It is murder (mosquitoes, of) before meditation.

It is the mock-grandeur of meditation, of honey
    suckle, baroque and bone.

It's the flight of the heron, the slow
    shift of light in Monaghan.

It is the quiet of Queen Anne's lace, of going
    alone in the lanes.

It is the lane lost among drumlins.

It is *go straight*, invariably straight, but the lane turns
    and the lane is always long.

It is the sorrow of Molly, of all dog.

It is the word *turfen*, the old word *bog*, Aghabog.

It is the church, not more than chapel, on the hill
    you must go the long way round to get to,
        merrily, merrily.

It is the abrupt dog Axel.

It is the Bible given to Susan Power
    by her mother in September
        1869.

It is the Psalter: dawn and desolation.

It is the uncovered love of David, loveliness
    gone of the Elizabethan
        word.

It is the bits of *persiflage* and *threnody*
    let softly slip by Bernard.

It is nonchalance.

It's silence, salt and bitter and good as soda bread.

Sunday afternoon at Maghera

I stare at the caves we've come too late to enter.

Already the sea is at home in them –
the strenuous, makeshift sea.

I am lost as to his need of me.

We walk in loneliness, the light
at Maghera

like milk spilt carefully.

We talk of five lost daughters, of his son, his own still,
undecidedly.

The sky makes shift.

I am afraid of Sunday.

I am afraid of the innocence of the sea.

turf
(for Marian)

the mountain silent after Phelim's gone

and ash like velvet on the hearthstone

and the comet with its great wind-sock of light

and ash like velvet, white

and shamrock, violet, hidden in the hedgebank by the stream

the bleak brown bogland

and the fire now slowly, slowly silting down

and ash that leaves our hands clean

neither one of us essential, neither one of us alone

Doon Fort

We have rowed round the bend in the lough to the island.
We have climbed. We have barely disturbed the dry, slant stones
of the fort. Or the late afternoon. Or the lough's rim,
root and stone. Beyond them, mountains.
Now the sun goes in. It is hard for us to be alone

with one another. Words have fled over the world's rim.
Imagination's fled. Is suddenly a simple wooden lid
that's lifted off to. Cloud reflected in the lough.
The silences of wind, of water. Swans, two pairs of,
their respective lough realms.

Inishkeel

Think of the unexpected helpfulness of water –

how it might strand you

on the small shore, here, as if this island were
the earth, its own frail sphere
of prayer

and obsolescence. There'd be tides and tides of
glittering small shells, broken here, like truths,
one after the other.

You'd be brevity, yourself barefoot.

You'd turn to salt as if you'd understood
the murmur of

the sea as missal. Yes, you might remember

gold or frankincense or myrrh –

you'd settle for the exhaled light of stars.

Sister Fidelma's Story

Lough Corrib came back to us, of course.
Father Cornelius said it would.
One day the land was inlaid with it again
Exactly where it should have been.

It must have come back on its own like a lost imagination.
No one was looking. Father Cornelius spoke of the moon
With its Lake of Dreams,
Lacus Somniorum.

Its reeds returned too and we knelt among them
In thanksgiving.

Then a paddleboat came proudly over the restored waters
Like a husband from Galway Town
To, as we thought, our own tidy household
Here in Annaghdown.

It cut across the wind with all its hatches open.
Water ran over its lower deck like a tongue.
'We are late, so late!' came a shout from its little megaphone.
'Please put the kettle on!'

TABITHA AND LINTEL

Things that are early

Lilith who lived before Eve
my birth, by five days
the cobweb across my path
illness in my mother's life, illness in my own
the wind on the downs
Maiden Castle
the star, before its own light, gone

Tabitha and Lintel: An Imaginary Tale

Until the day break, and the shadows flee away,
I will get me to the mountain of myrrh,
And to the hill of frankincense.

THE SONG OF SONGS, 4.6

Taby said on my putting a pen in her face Ya pitter pottering
there instead of pilling a potate

EMILY BRONTË's *Diary Paper,*
Monday 24th November 1834

LINTEL

Who is it, then, that imagines me out of my mountain lair
and into the habit of hovering, here, at the doorstone,
mornings, in the slant new sun, the cobwebs covering
a whole field like a shroud of butter muslin
woven, light and water, like a poem
coming quietly into being?
                              Is it Tabitha, my singing
Tabitha, for whom I am become a habit of the tongue
and telling? Tabitha named me. Tabitha brings me
bread she's broken from a corner of the nuns' new loaf.
She'll ask me for the story of my life.
Snails have crossed the doorstone in the dark night
secretly as nuns, at compline, in procession.
Tabitha brought me an old brown habit to wrap myself in.
She'll tell me there are too many steps between the kitchen
and her attic room. Tabitha has a narrow bed, a candle
and a mat to kneel on.
                      Later, when the sun goes down
I'll get me to the mountain, walking through the water-meadow
to the narrow wooden bridge, breaking off
bits of bread and eating them.
                              Whoever imagines me into
my story doesn't know who I am or why I won't come in —
though Tabitha bids me not be so alone.

Tabitha, arise I tell myself these late September mornings
when the light is shroud-thin and the moon – or maybe
there is no moon – and Mother Superior told me the story
of Tabitha, the other one. And Peter came, she said, *and all
the widows stood by him weeping, and shewing the coats and
garments which Dorcas made, while she was with them.*
Dorcas must have been my other name. A sister.
Tabitha, arise I tell the leavened bread.
It'll be fat as a clay pot or the thought of God –
and *Take it, eat it while it's hot* I'll say –
not like the little paper loaf they lift from the altar
and place on the tongue, as if it were a leaf, an autumn
leaf, a lone moon – thin the word *life*, as they say it,
insubstantial. I must have imagined that girl.
Whoever imagines me must want some sewing done.
Coats and garments – that was the other one. Make do and mend
in perpetuity, me, and the thread like broken string.
Wool cloth for the habits, calico the Lenten petticoats,
the linen underthings. Only the shrouds of lightest butter muslin.
Tabitha, rise and take the little loaf to her.
                                        Undo
the bolted door while all the sisters are at prayer.

LINTEL

Whoever imagines Lintel lifted her out of the *Flower Fairy*
    Alphabet Book.

Whoever imagines, met once, as it had been innocence, a midden
of worn shoes in a wooden hut, Maidanek,

and hasn't forgotten the smell of creosote.

Tabitha's sandals remind her of her old school corridor.

Tabitha met me, the first time, walking in the lane.
She was carrying letters for Mother Superior.

I didn't invent her, who, in the tale, will turn out to be
my adoptive godmother, childless Tabitha, she who imagined
her own immaculate conception and sewed a layette.
There was even a shroud for it.

I've a lair of my own without lions or nuns. Whoever imagines

me, may remember herself in a gaberdine coat and hat
lined up on the asphalt drive of the convent school
to see the Queen Mother – or was it Princess Margaret?
A day in September, clouded over, cool.

She's almost forgotten it.

My orphan, own girl, Lintel: the sea at the door.
I could not imagine her otherwise. The Holy Land
is hard and dry as the moon with its own dour
sea of serenity, *Mare Serenitatis*, Mother Superior's
tongue, the nuns at the end of their tether,
the end of their prayer Gethsemane, Golgotha.
Hers is the sea and the sea's is the last shroud
laid in the press.
                    Whoever imagines, wants
me reeled, like thread, a stop short of timelessness,
wants me to kneel on the mat by the narrow bed
in prayer and then, with *Tabitha, rise*, get up
from the unforgiving floor to gather the stars
in my arms, remember Lintel in her lair
and say *God bless her.*
                    Why dismiss her so?
The death of the other, my sister as if, my own dear
Dorcas with her *coats and garments*, opened
me to that which was and is
mysterious.
                    I'll not betray her with a mere *God bless.*

LINTEL

Whoever imagines me thinks of the arkhold, Ararat.

God, in naming it and Noah, let the unimaginable sink
the wife of Noah, naked, in a sea of anonymity, *Mare
Anonymitatis.*
        Whoever she was went untold, tameless
as the waters.

Mine is the arcane mountain of motherlessness, immeasurable
meditation.

Here the stars are undeterred.
        I have myself disinterred the stars.

Tabitha, halfway up or down her convent stairs,
may not applaud me.
        Coats and garments she muttered yesterday morning.
She's said it so often, as if it were part of her prayer
or the telling over of beads they do there.

The stars are yarrow seeds or burrs that stick to the habit
of walking.
        I saw them
stuck to the shawl, to the indoor shoes of the newly widowed
woman I met walking in the lane.

TABITHA

Stars come in shoals these cold September nights.

She flits now, four fields off, a light wind
hollowing her habit, as if she were all sail
and hardly a boat to bear it.
                    She will not be harboured
though I wait here, longing and looking out over the low hedgerows
for her, the bread in a cloth. It won't cool yet.

Loaves and fishes Mother Superior said.

The stars in shoals, the bread for Lintel in a disused shawl.

Now she sculls carefully over the cattle-grid at the convent
gate.
                Now she sculls home, as I'd have it, home.

The hem of her habit is wet.

And how shall I gather the sea in my arms?

LINTEL

Whoever imagines me went most reluctantly to school.

I feel it in the soles of my feet walking over the wide
lid of Hell, though the cattle-grid bars burn cold
this morning, cold as the lid of the stove
or love gone out a week, a century, ago.
                                        Tabitha will
have nothing to do with the harrowing of Hell.

She wants me to walk in there, like Daniel.

She wants me to wear sandals.

Tabitha's full of tales.
                        She tells me I could bring in coal.
The scuttles are small and it's only the parlour, Mother Superior's
O and the big hall just at Christmas – where the fires are lit at all.
The nuns wear wool in winter and there's many a tale of
wickedness to warm the edges of the soul.

Tell me a wicked tale I'll say. *My feet are cold.*

How beautiful are thy feet with shoes
she'll say *or could be. Look at them –*
black as the bars of the cattle-grid but comely.

TABITHA

Maidanek, a middenstead, a mountain, enclosed, of shoes.

I put on our shoes as Mother Superior said the mad monk
    Thomas Merton said.

Whoever imagined my soul unmolested by love shall be interred.

Lintel can have the small guest bed.

The air of the parlour's been breathed already by Mother Superior.
It is crumpled and warm, like a bed. It has lost the austere
queer shroud of itself, of the room before morning
prayer. The shadows have fled.
                    I've to mend the fire
once more in there where the air is like Limbo.
In Limbo they live on stale bread and sorrow she said.
And there, as yesterday, will be Our Lady of Perpetual Tears
and a pile of letters under the paperweight
and Mother Superior with her heart inside her
habit, like an old brown teapot, breathing the air.
And I will murmur *Stella Maris, Stella Maris*
as Tabitha told me, *Star of the Sea.*

It'll be as if I'd brought the breakers in with me.

*   *   *

Healer

(for Nansi Morgan)

Like the heart or the mountain painted again
and again by Cézanne,

she will not mind what I mean
to myself or anyone.

To her, as to wind, sand and stars
or Mont Sainte-Victoire,

I shall come to learn
to be alone,

articulate. She will allow me to listen.

She will allow me to live without consolation.

things that are early and late

'the gold of the earls'
this pelican's foot shell
my own heart, hobbled by an unexpected tale
at eleven o'clock, a light meal
the moment of the sparrow in the meadhall
music written later, we think, for the sackbut or the viol
'this hardened helmet healed with gold'

A Letter from Marie-Claire to Her Sister: Though Marie-Claire and the events she refers to are entirely fictional, something of the life and work of Gwen John inhabits the poem.

Her Father in the Patients' Garden, Newcastle Borough Lunatic Asylum, 1919: The hospital, taken over by the Ministry of War during the First World War, is now known as St Nicholas' Hospital.

Awkward Things (2): 'Crossing the Desert in a Pram' is the title of a poem by Selima Hill.

Arvo Pärt in Concert, Durham Cathedral, November 1998: The lines in italics are taken from the text of Arvo Pärt's *Litany*, a setting of the 24 prayers attributed to St John Chrysostom for each hour of the day and night. St John Chrysostom, a hermit, became Patriarch of Constantinople in 398.

While Cuthbert, born in 634, was a monk at Melrose Abbey, he visited the religious house at Coldingham, and it was there, according to legend, that he stood all night in the sea and in the morning was warmed by seals. From 664 he was Prior of Lindisfarne and, while Prior, spent three years living as a hermit on one of the nearby Farne Islands. In 685, against his will, he was made Bishop of Lindisfarne. He died and was buried there in 687. Because of Viking raids, the monks took Cuthbert's coffin and embarked in 873 on 'the wanderings', continuing until a final resting-place was found for the saint in 995, on the site of the present Durham Cathedral, which still contains his shrine.

Tabitha and Lintel: An Imaginary Tale: Tabitha is the housekeeper in a convent. Lintel is a girl of about nine who comes every morning to the convent door and is given bread. The story of Tabitha can be found in *Acts*, 9. 36-43. *A Flower Fairy Alphabet Book* by Cicely Mary Barker was first published in 1934. Maidanek, a Nazi camp in Eastern Poland, is now a museum. Thomas Merton (1915-68) was a Trappist monk and writer.

things that are early and late: Quoted lines are from *Beowulf*, translated by Michael Alexander.